I0099030

PRAYERSCRIPTS
Speaking God's Word Back To You

PEACE
THROUGH THE
BLOOD

60 DAYS OF PRAYERS FOR
RESTING IN THE COVENANT OF
UNSHAKABLE PEACE

CYRIL OPOKU

Peace Through the Blood: 60 Days of Prayers for Resting in the Covenant of Unshakable Peace

© 2025 Cyril Opoku. *PrayerScripts*. All rights reserved.

No part of this publication may be reproduced, stored in a retrieval system, or transmitted in any form or by any means—electronic, mechanical, photocopy, recording, or otherwise—without the prior written permission of the publisher, except in the case of brief quotations used in reviews, articles, or devotionals.

Published by *Quest Publications*

ISBN: 978-1-988439-73-0

Cover design by *Quest Publications (questpublications@outlook.com)*

Unless otherwise indicated, all Scripture quotations are taken from the World English Bible WEB, which is in the public domain. For more information, visit: www.worldenglish.bible

This book is a work of devotional encouragement. It is not intended to replace biblical study, pastoral counsel, or professional therapy.

Printed in the United States of America.

First Edition: August 2025

For more books like this, visit *PrayerScripts:* https://prayerscripts.org

CONTENTS

PREFACE

"Having made peace through the blood of his cross..."
— Colossians 1:20 WEB

The pursuit of peace in our day has become an urgent necessity. Anxiety has become a silent epidemic, relationships are often strained, and the constant noise of the world makes stillness feel out of reach. Yet for the believer, peace is not a fleeting feeling to be chased—it is a covenant right, sealed by the blood of Jesus Christ. This book was birthed from that unshakable truth.

Peace Through the Blood is the sixth volume in *The Blood Covenant Series*, and it was written with one purpose: to guide you into experiencing the mental, emotional, and relational rest that was purchased for you at the cross. Colossians 1:20 declares that Christ *"made peace through the blood of his cross."* This is not poetic language—it is the reality of a transaction that has already been completed in heaven and made available to you here on earth.

These 60 daily prayers are prophetic in nature, speaking directly to your spirit and activating faith for peace that defies circumstances. Each prayer is rooted in Scripture, framed through the lens of the blood covenant, and crafted to draw you into a deeper experience of God's presence.

As you pray, you will learn to silence the storms within, break the grip of fear, heal emotional wounds, and see God's peace flow into your relationships. This is not a peace you manufacture—it is a peace you receive, protect, and walk in as your covenant inheritance.

My prayer is that this book becomes more than words on a page. May it be a living guide, a daily altar, and a lasting wellspring from which you and your household drink deeply of the unshakable peace of God.

In the unshakable peace of Christ,

Cyril O. *(Illinois, August 2025)*

INTRODUCTION

The night Jesus faced betrayal, He told His disciples, *"Peace I leave with you. My peace I give to you; not as the world gives, give I to you"* (John 14:27 WEB). That statement carries the weight of eternity. It was not merely a farewell blessing—it was the bequeathing of His own peace as a permanent possession for His followers. And the means by which He would secure it was the shedding of His blood.

When we think of the blood of Jesus, our minds often go first to forgiveness, and rightly so. But the same blood that pardoned us also purchased our peace. Through it, every wall of hostility between God and man was torn down. Through it, our souls were anchored to the unchanging faithfulness of God. Through it, the storms of the mind and the chaos of the heart meet their Master and fall silent.

This book exists because too many of God's people live without truly knowing that this peace is already theirs. We've mistaken peace for the absence of problems, but biblical peace—*shalom*—is much deeper. It means wholeness, safety, health, and harmony. It means being so complete in God's presence that nothing is missing, broken, or out of order.

In these pages, you will find daily prayers that are not timid requests but bold prophetic decrees rooted in the authority of the blood. You will speak peace over your mind, your emotions, your relationships, and your home—not because you hope it will come, but because Jesus has already signed it into your inheritance.

Let every page remind you: Peace is not just God's gift to you; it is His will for you. And His will is sealed in blood.

How to Use This Book

This is not a book to be rushed through. Each of the 60 prayers is designed as a focused encounter—an intentional moment to align your spirit, soul, and body with the reality of peace through the blood of Jesus Christ.

Here's a suggested way to walk through it:

1. **Set Your Atmosphere** – Begin each day by finding a quiet place, free from distraction. If possible, play soft instrumental worship that draws your heart to the Lord.

2. **Read the Scripture Aloud** – Each prayer begins with a verse from the World English Bible (WEB). Speak it out loud, letting the Word wash over your mind.

3. **Pray Prophetically** – These prayers are written in the first person so you can pray them as your own. Declare them with faith, not as wishful thinking, but as truth you are enforcing over your life and family.

4. **Personalize the Decrees** – As you pray, insert specific names, situations, or relationships where you want God's peace to reign.

5. **Meditate and Journal** – After praying, write down any impressions, Scriptures, or breakthroughs you sense. This will build a record of God's faithfulness.

6. **Revisit as Needed** – Some prayers will speak to you beyond a single day. Don't hesitate to repeat them until you see full manifestation.

This book is also suited for family devotion, prayer groups, or corporate gatherings. Speaking these words together can amplify their impact and cultivate a shared atmosphere of peace.

Above all, approach these prayers with expectation. The blood of Jesus is not a mere symbol—it is living, speaking, and powerful. As you walk through these 60 days, you are not striving for peace; you are receiving and enforcing what the cross has already secured.

DAY 1

PEACE PURCHASED AT THE CROSS

"Having made peace through the blood of his cross..."
— Colossians 1:20 WEB

O Prince of Peace, I lift my heart to You in holy gratitude, for Your blood has spoken a better word over my life and my household. At the cross, You did not merely purchase my pardon—you secured my peace, a covenant peace that storms cannot steal and enemies cannot overthrow. I declare over my mind, my emotions, and my relationships: the peace of God, bought with the crimson price, rules here.

Lord Jesus, let the power of Your blood silence every voice of fear, unrest, and confusion. May Your peace flow like a river through my home, calming anxious hearts, soothing wounded spirits, and knitting us together in Your unfailing love. Let every spiritual storm dissipate under the weight of this covenant truth: I am reconciled to God, and therefore, I am secure.

I stand in the unshakable reality that my peace is not fragile or circumstantial—it is anchored in the finished work of the cross. Every dark cloud of strife must part, for the blood has decreed my wholeness. I embrace this peace for me, my family, and generations to come.

In Jesus' name, Amen.

DAY 2

Inner Peace, My Right in Christ

"Being justified by faith, we have peace with God…"
— Romans 5:1 WEB

Faithful Father, I boldly declare that I have been justified through faith in the Lord Jesus Christ. This is not a temporary verdict but an eternal decree, and with it comes the peace that flows from being in right standing with You. No guilt, shame, or accusation can overthrow this peace, for it is my covenant right in Christ.

Let this divine peace flood my inner being and the atmosphere of my home. Lord, drive out the unrest that seeks to lodge in our minds and emotions. Replace every burden with the ease of Your presence, every tension with the stillness of Your Spirit. Let the peace of God be the air my family breathes, the shield around our hearts, and the foundation under our feet.

I proclaim that our peace is not subject to the shifting sands of life's pressures. It is rooted in Christ's unchanging love and the eternal verdict of "justified." This peace guards us, strengthens us, and guides us into every good work You have prepared. We receive it now as our portion.

In Jesus' name, Amen.

DAY 3

PEACE WITH GOD THROUGH JUSTIFICATION

"Much more then, being now justified by his blood…"
— Romans 5:9 WEB

Righteous Judge, I stand under the covering of the blood that justifies. You have pronounced me righteous, not by my deeds, but by the perfect sacrifice of Jesus Christ. Because of this, I have peace with You—a peace that banishes every fear of judgment and reconciles my heart to Yours.

Let the power of justification through the blood saturate my soul and my family's life. Wash away every lingering shadow of condemnation, every whisper of inadequacy, and every lie of the enemy that seeks to steal our rest. Let this peace anchor us in the certainty that we are loved, accepted, and secure in Your presence.

Lord, I receive this blood-bought peace as a shield for my home. May it guard our minds in anxious moments, protect our hearts from offense, and knit our relationships together in grace. This is the heritage of the justified: peace with God and wholeness in every part of life. I claim it for me and my household.

In Jesus' name, Amen.

DAY 4

THE BLOOD SILENCES SEPARATION ANXIETY

"But now in Christ Jesus you who once were far off are
made near in the blood of Christ. For he is our peace..."
— Ephesians 2:13-14 WEB

Covenant-Keeping God, I rejoice that by the blood of Jesus, I am no longer far from You. The distance sin created has been forever closed, and in its place stands a bond of unbreakable nearness. You Yourself are my peace, and I rest in Your presence.

Lord, silence every fear of abandonment, rejection, and isolation in my life and my family. Let the power of the blood speak louder than the voices that say we are alone. Surround our hearts with the tangible reality of Your nearness. Let my home be a dwelling place for Your peace, where no spirit of separation or division can find entrance.

I declare that the blood of Christ has brought us near, not just to You but to one another. In this nearness, there is healing for wounds, restoration for broken connections, and strength for the journey ahead. Your peace is not distant—it is here, alive, and reigning in our midst.

In Jesus' name, Amen.

DAY 5

PAID-IN-FULL PEACE FOR MY SOUL

"…the chastisement of our peace was on him…"
— Isaiah 53:5 WEB

Lamb of God, I worship You for taking upon Yourself the chastisement that purchased my peace. Every stripe, every wound, every moment of suffering was the price for my wholeness—and You paid it in full. I will not accept anything less than what You died to give me.

Let this paid-in-full peace govern my soul and my household. Where there has been turmoil, let there now be rest. Where there has been fear, let there be faith. Let my mind be still, my emotions be steady, and my relationships be clothed in harmony because of what You endured for me.

I declare that no storm will override the peace secured by Your sacrifice. My family walks in the freedom of a soul unshaken by the enemy's lies. This peace is our legal inheritance, and we receive it with gratitude and boldness, knowing it cost You everything.

In Jesus' name, Amen.

DAY 6

PEACE IN A CLEAN AND HEALED CONSCIENCE

"...how much more will the blood of Christ... purge your
conscience from dead works to serve the living God?"
— Hebrews 9:14 WEB

Holy Redeemer, I thank You for the blood of Jesus that not only washes away my sins but cleanses my conscience. You have lifted the heavy weight of guilt and replaced it with the lightness of peace. I am free to serve You with a heart unburdened and a mind at rest.

Lord, let this cleansing reach into every corner of my soul and into the hearts of my family. Heal the hidden wounds, silence the accusing memories, and uproot the seeds of shame. Let us stand before You with clear consciences, fully persuaded that we are accepted in the Beloved.

May this peace flow into our daily lives, making service to You a joy and not a duty, and relationships a blessing and not a strain. Let the atmosphere of our home reflect the purity of a conscience cleansed by the blood—light, open, and full of Your glory.

In Jesus' name, Amen.

DAY 7

THE PEACE OF BEING FULLY CLEANSED

"…to him who loves us, and washed us from our sins by
his blood…"
— Revelation 1:5 WEB

Faithful Savior, I lift my voice in gratitude to the One who loves me
and has washed me clean in His blood. No stain remains, no record
stands against me. Your cleansing is complete, and with it comes a
peace that no defilement can disturb.

Lord, let this truth saturate my soul and my household. May we live
in the liberty of the cleansed, free from the chains of shame and the
burden of regret. Let our peace be deep, settled, and constant—
rooted in the knowledge that we are spotless before You.

I declare that every lie of the enemy that tries to accuse us falls
powerless at the mention of Your blood. We are loved, we are
washed, and we are at rest in the assurance of our salvation. This
peace reigns in our hearts and in our home, unshaken by past
failures or present challenges.

In Jesus' name, Amen.

DAY 8

WALKING DAILY IN CLEANSING PEACE

"...and the blood of Jesus Christ, his Son, cleanses us from
all sin."
— 1 John 1:7 WEB

Eternal King, I praise You for the ongoing, daily cleansing of the
blood of Jesus. This is not a one-time work, but a continual flow that
keeps me and my family pure, free, and at peace. Each step I take is
under the covering of this cleansing river.

Lord, let this daily cleansing guard our hearts from the build-up of
offense, bitterness, or regret. As You wash us anew each day, fill us
with fresh peace—peace that flows unhindered because no sin is
left to trouble our consciences. Let this be the rhythm of our home:
walk in the light, receive the cleansing, live in the peace.

I declare that my household will not be weighed down by the
residue of yesterday. The blood of Jesus cleanses today, tomorrow,
and every day after. We will walk in this continual peace, free to love
You and one another with unclouded hearts.

In Jesus' name, Amen.

DAY 9

PEACE THROUGH FORGIVENESS

"Blessed is he whose disobedience is forgiven, whose sin
is covered."
— Psalm 32:1 WEB

Merciful Father, I bless Your name for the joy and peace that come
from being forgiven. My sins are not exposed for judgment—they
are covered by the blood of the Lamb. This covering is my shelter,
my safety, and my song.

Lord, let this forgiveness shape the atmosphere of my home. Where
there is forgiveness, there is peace; where there is peace, there is
unity; and where there is unity, Your presence dwells. Let the reality
of covered sin free us from defensiveness, soften our words, and
deepen our love for one another.

I declare that my family will not live under the weight of past
failures. We are the blessed of the Lord—washed, covered, and at
rest in His mercy. This peace is not fragile; it is built on the
immovable truth of divine pardon.

In Jesus' name, Amen.

DAY 10

Peace in Chaos from Faith in the Blood

"...whom God set forth to be an atoning sacrifice, through faith in his blood..."
— Romans 3:25 WEB

Mighty God, I put my faith fully in the blood of Jesus. This blood is my anchor when the waves of life rise high, my shield when chaos rages around me. Because of this blood, I have peace that defies understanding and overrules fear.

Lord, in every situation that threatens my calm—whether in my mind, my emotions, or my relationships—let my faith in the blood speak louder than the storm. May my household be a place where the chaos outside cannot invade, for the peace within is guarded by divine covenant.

I declare that the blood of Jesus is my family's defense, our assurance, and our peace in every circumstance. We do not look to the instability of the world; we rest in the eternal stability of the cross. Our faith in the blood releases heaven's peace right here, right now.

In Jesus' name, Amen.

DAY 11

CALM CONFIDENCE IN GOD'S PRESENCE

"Let's draw near with a true heart in fullness of faith,
having our hearts sprinkled from an evil conscience, and
having our body washed with pure water."
— Hebrews 10:22 WEB

O Faithful Father, I come boldly into Your presence today, knowing that the blood of Jesus has cleansed my conscience from every stain of guilt and fear. By that precious blood, my heart has been sprinkled clean, and my spirit now rises above the whispers of condemnation. I declare that my family and I are free to draw near to You with full assurance, unshaken and unafraid, for the peace of Your presence is our resting place.

Lord of Peace, the storms of doubt cannot stand before the calm of Your Spirit. You have silenced every accusation and replaced it with the stillness of Your love. In this sanctuary of grace, I declare over my household that we will walk in unbroken communion with You—confident, steadfast, and secure.

By the power of the blood, our minds are settled, our emotions are stilled, and our hearts are anchored in the knowledge of Your favor. I decree that the peace of God's nearness will be the atmosphere of our home, now and forever. In Jesus' name, Amen.

DAY 12

Hearing the Voice of Peace

"I will hear what God, Yahweh, will speak, for he will speak
peace to his people, his saints; but let them not turn again
to folly."
— Psalm 85:8 WEB

Prince of Peace, I still my heart before You, for the voice of the blood speaks louder than the noise of the world. Your Word declares that You speak peace to Your people, and I receive that promise over my life and my family today. Every anxious thought, every restless feeling, bows to the sound of Your calming voice.

Through the blood of Jesus, You silence the lies of the enemy and speak wholeness to our spirits. You remind us that we are Yours—redeemed, beloved, and safe in the shadow of Your wings. I decree that every member of my household will hear and obey the voice of the Lord, walking in wisdom and never returning to paths of destruction.

Your peace is not fragile; it is fortified by the eternal covenant of the cross. I declare that this peace will govern our decisions, shape our relationships, and preserve our unity. The blood has spoken, and we say "Amen" to every word of blessing and rest You release over us. In Jesus' name, Amen.

DAY 13

PEACE THROUGH RESURRECTION POWER

"Now may the God of peace, who brought again from the
dead the great shepherd of the sheep with the blood of an
eternal covenant, our Lord Jesus…"
— Hebrews 13:20 WEB

God of Resurrection, I lift my voice in praise, for the same blood
that sealed the eternal covenant is the blood that brought Jesus from
the dead. That power is working in my life today to restore every
peace I have lost. Where sorrow tried to linger, joy is breaking forth.
Where confusion clouded my mind, clarity now reigns.

Great Shepherd, You lead my family beside still waters and restore
our souls. The blood of the covenant has reclaimed what the enemy
tried to steal—our calm, our unity, our hope. We are not bound to
yesterday's losses, for resurrection life flows through us.

I decree that by the blood, every dead area in our relationships,
emotions, and dreams comes alive again. The peace we walk in is
not fragile, for it is rooted in the victory of the empty tomb. We rise
today in boldness and serenity, knowing our lives are secured in
Your covenant care. In Jesus' name, Amen.

DAY 14

Peace in Full Redemption

"In whom we have our redemption through his blood, the forgiveness of our trespasses, according to the riches of his grace."
— Ephesians 1:7 WEB

Redeeming Lord, I rejoice that the blood of Jesus has purchased my full release from sin and its torment. No shadow of guilt can stand before the light of Your grace. I declare over my life and my family that our peace is untouchable, for it rests on the unshakable foundation of redemption.

In this holy covenant, You have erased every accusation and made us whole. Your grace floods our hearts with quiet strength, teaching us to rest in the certainty that we are forgiven and free. The storms of the past have no voice in our present, for the blood has spoken "It is finished."

I decree that my household will live in the richness of Your grace, walking in rest, joy, and security. The peace of full redemption will guard our hearts, heal our wounds, and bless our days. In Jesus' name, Amen.

DAY 15

A Renewed Mind for Peace

"For the mind of the flesh is death, but the mind of the
Spirit is life and peace."
— Romans 8:6 WEB

Spirit of Truth, I yield my thoughts to You, for the blood of Jesus
has broken the chains of carnal thinking. I receive the mind of
Christ—a mind filled with life and peace. Over my family and me,
I declare that we will think in harmony with Heaven, guided by
Your Word and not by fear.

Through the covenant blood, every toxic thought pattern is
uprooted, and every lie is replaced with the truth of God's promises.
Our minds are renewed, our emotions settled, and our hearts
aligned with Your purposes. Life and peace flow like a river through
our home.

I decree that we will not be moved by the chaos of the world, but
will dwell in the stillness that comes from being spiritually minded.
The blood of the Lamb has secured for us this priceless gift, and we
will guard it faithfully. In Jesus' name, Amen.

DAY 16

PEACE AS MY INHERITANCE

"Peace I leave with you. My peace I give to you; not as the
world gives, I give to you. Don't let your heart be troubled,
neither let it be fearful."
— John 14:27 WEB

Jesus, my Covenant King, I embrace the peace You have left for
me—a peace sealed and secured by Your blood. This is no fragile
calm that shatters under pressure, but a heavenly stillness that
steadies my soul. I declare that my family and I will live in this
inheritance daily, unmoved by fear, untouched by turmoil.

Your peace is a treasure the world cannot give or take away. It
guards my heart, settles my mind, and establishes our home in
divine rest. I choose to release every burden into Your hands, for
the blood testifies that our victory is complete.

I decree that our hearts will remain untroubled and fearless, for we
are anchored in the covenant of peace. No storm can shake what
the cross has secured. In Jesus' name, Amen.

DAY 17

Perfect Peace in Trust

"You will keep whoever's mind is steadfast in perfect peace, because he trusts in you."
— Isaiah 26:3 WEB

Faithful Keeper, I set my trust fully upon You. The blood of Jesus has made me Your own, and You have pledged to keep me in perfect peace. I declare that my mind is steadfast, unshaken by shifting circumstances, for my hope rests in the covenant.

Over my household, I speak stability. We will not be tossed about by fear or uncertainty, for our trust is in the unchanging God of peace. Your Spirit steadies our hearts, and Your blood speaks a continual assurance that we are safe in Your hands.

I decree that our thoughts will remain fixed on You, our words filled with faith, and our atmosphere saturated with peace. We walk in this promise as our inheritance. In Jesus' name, Amen.

DAY 18

PEACE GUARDING MY EMOTIONS

"The peace of God, which surpasses all understanding,
will guard your hearts and your thoughts in Christ Jesus."
— Philippians 4:7 WEB

Lord of Glory, I welcome the peace that comes from Your throne—
a peace that surpasses understanding and shields my heart like a
fortress. By the blood of Jesus, this peace is mine and my family's to
dwell in forever.

Your peace guards our emotions from the attacks of anxiety, anger,
or fear. It stands like sentinels around our minds, ensuring that we
think and feel according to Your truth. Through the covenant
blood, I declare that every troubling thought is cast down, and
every wave of unrest is calmed.

I decree that our hearts are fortified in Christ Jesus, immune to the
enemy's disruptions. The peace of God will remain our constant
companion, a blood-bought shield for every season. In Jesus' name,
Amen.

DAY 19

SANCTIFIED IN THE PEACE OF THE BLOOD

"...in sanctification of the Spirit, that you may obey Jesus
Christ and be sprinkled with his blood..."
— 1 Peter 1:2 WEB

Holy and Righteous God, I thank You that the blood of Jesus has been sprinkled over my life, setting me apart for Your purposes. This blood speaks peace into my soul and consecrates my family to live in the beauty of holiness.

In this sanctifying peace, we are empowered to obey You without fear. The turmoil of sin is broken, the chaos of rebellion is silenced, and the tranquility of Your Spirit fills our home. By the blood, we are not only forgiven—we are transformed.

I decree that my household will walk in this holy peace daily, manifesting the joy and rest that comes from living set apart for You. We are kept in the covenant by the sprinkled blood, and nothing shall disturb our harmony. In Jesus' name, Amen.

DAY 20

PEACE IN GOD'S HOLY PRESENCE

"Having therefore, brothers, boldness to enter into the holy place by the blood of Jesus…"
— Hebrews 10:19 WEB

Majestic King, I rejoice that the blood of Jesus has opened the way into Your holy presence. With boldness, I enter today—not as a stranger, but as a beloved child. Here in Your presence, peace flows like a river and fills every part of my being.

This peace is not fleeting; it is born from the assurance that I belong to You. I declare that my family will live with this same holy boldness, drawing near daily to the throne of grace. The closer we are to You, the deeper our peace becomes.

By the covenant blood, fear is banished, guilt is erased, and rest is restored. We will remain in this place of communion, letting Your presence be the source and sustainer of our peace. In Jesus' name, Amen.

DAY 21

PEACE AS MY WARFARE WEAPON

"They overcame him because of the Lamb's blood, and because of the word of their testimony. They didn't love their life, even to death."
— Revelation 12:11 WEB

Almighty God, Captain of my salvation, I lift my voice today in the authority of the blood of Jesus. The enemy's schemes are silenced, his accusations shattered, and his strategies overthrown, for the blood has already secured my victory. Through this holy blood, I receive Your peace as a weapon—a divine force that crushes confusion, disarms fear, and drives back the darkness from me and my family.

I declare that every storm sent to disrupt our minds, our emotions, or our relationships is met with the stillness of Heaven's shalom. The peace purchased by the blood is not passive; it is a militant calm, a ruling force that breaks the back of chaos. This peace shields our home, surrounds our hearts, and keeps us unshaken in the face of battle.

By the testimony of Christ in my life, I announce that my family walks in triumph. No evil can prevail against the sound of the blood that covers us, and no fear can withstand the peace that floods us. We stand victorious, resting in the covenant that will never fail.

In Jesus' name, Amen.

DAY 22

ANCHORED IN CHRIST'S FINISHED PEACE

"I have told you these things, that in me you may have peace. In the world you have oppression; but cheer up! I have overcome the world."
— John 16:33 WEB

Lord Jesus, Prince of Peace, I anchor my soul in the harbor of Your victory. You have spoken, and Your word is unshakable: in You I have peace, not as the world gives, but as Heaven supplies. This peace is anchored in the unchangeable truth that You have already overcome every trial, temptation, and torment that could rise against me and my household.

Though the waves of life roar and the winds howl, I refuse to drift into fear or despair. Your finished work is my mooring; the blood of the cross is my proof. You have subdued every enemy, conquered every threat, and disarmed every weapon of the wicked.

Therefore, I lay my family's hearts, minds, and futures in Your steady hands. We choose cheer in the face of pressure, because the Victor Himself dwells within us. Peace flows like a river through our home, silencing anxiety, calming our thoughts, and keeping us steadfast. We are hidden in You, and in You, we are unmovable.

In Jesus' name, Amen.

DAY 23

RESTING IN THE UNSHAKABLE COVENANT

"For the mountains may depart, and the hills be removed;
but my loving kindness will not depart from you, and my
covenant of peace will not be removed," says Yahweh who
has mercy on you.
— Isaiah 54:10 WEB

Faithful Covenant Keeper, my heart bows in awe of Your unbreakable promise. The mountains may tremble, the very ground may shift, but the covenant of peace sealed in the blood of Jesus will never fail. It stands eternal, unshaken by time, trial, or the threats of the enemy.

I rest my life and my family in the stronghold of this peace. When the world shakes with instability, we stand on the foundation of Your mercy. Your covenant does not shift with circumstances; it is rooted in the blood that forever speaks on our behalf.

Lord, we refuse to be moved by the instability around us. We dwell in the shelter of Your covenant love, confident that no power can remove the peace You have decreed over us. Let this divine calm guard our hearts, saturate our relationships, and steady our emotions every day of our lives.

In Jesus' name, Amen.

DAY 24

THE PEACE OF HIS LIFTED FACE

"Yahweh lift up his face toward you, and give you peace."
— Numbers 6:26 WEB

Abba Father, when Your face shines upon me, every shadow flees. Through the blood of Jesus, I stand in the light of Your countenance, embraced by Your gaze of love. In that holy presence, my fears dissolve, my heart stills, and my mind finds perfect rest.

I invite the fullness of this peace over my family today. Let the light of Your lifted face break through every cloud of heaviness, driving away oppression and weariness. Where there has been tension, release harmony; where there has been confusion, release clarity; where there has been unrest, release stillness.

Lord, we live beneath Your blessing. Your peace is not a passing moment—it is our continual covering. As You look upon us with favor, may the fragrance of Your presence linger in our home, drawing us ever deeper into Your embrace.

In Jesus' name, Amen.

DAY 25

PEACE AS MY DIVINE BLESSING

"Yahweh will give strength to his people. Yahweh will bless
his people with peace."
— Psalm 29:11 WEB

Mighty God, You are my Strength and my Shield. Today I lift my
hands in thanksgiving for the blessing of peace that flows from Your
throne, secured for me through the blood of the Lamb. This is not
the peace the world offers—it is Heaven's own substance, breathed
into my spirit and my home.

Lord, let this blessing saturate my family's hearts. May it be strength
to the weary, calm to the troubled, and courage to the faint. Let Your
peace guard the doors of our minds and the gates of our
relationships, driving out every intruder of fear, strife, and unrest.

We stand in the full assurance that this peace is a gift from You—
unchangeable, irrevocable, and unending. It is the climate of
Heaven made manifest in our lives. We walk in it, we rest in it, and
we war with it, knowing that peace is our heritage.

In Jesus' name, Amen.

DAY 26

THE BLOOD SPEAKS PEACE

"...and to Jesus, the mediator of a new covenant, and to the blood of sprinkling that speaks better than that of Abel."
— Hebrews 12:24 WEB

Lord Jesus, Mediator of my covenant, I thank You for the blood that speaks louder than accusation, louder than fear, and louder than the storms that rage around me. Your blood speaks peace—a peace so deep it subdues every force of darkness.

Today, I bring my family under the sound of that voice. Let the declaration of Your blood silence every shout of confusion, cancel every whisper of anxiety, and break every echo of past pain. Let its proclamation be heard in every corner of our lives: "Peace, be still."

We yield to this holy announcement. We live under the constant proclamation of mercy, restoration, and calm. Your blood does not merely speak in the heavens; it speaks here, now, in our hearts and in our home. We agree with its testimony, and we walk in its unshakable peace.

In Jesus' name, Amen.

DAY 27

GRACE AND PEACE THROUGH THE CROSS

"Now about the things which I write to you, behold, before
God, I'm not lying."
— Galatians 1:20 WEB

God of all grace, I receive the flow of Your grace and peace made
mine through the crucified Christ. This peace is not earned; it is
gifted, purchased with holy blood and secured in an everlasting
covenant.

Let this grace lift every weight from my shoulders and dissolve
every tension in my spirit. Let this peace, born from the cross,
anchor my emotions and safeguard my thoughts. Lord, may my
family walk in the rhythm of grace, free from the push and pull of
fear.

We stand in the reality that grace has brought us near, and peace
has made us whole. Through the power of the blood, we reject the
turbulence of this world and embrace the stillness of Your presence.

In Jesus' name, Amen.

DAY 28

THE LIFE OF PEACE IN THE BLOOD

"For the life of the flesh is in the blood; and I have given it
to you on the altar to make atonement for your souls: for
it is the blood that makes atonement by reason of the life."
— Leviticus 17:11 WEB

Eternal God, I thank You for the life that flows through the blood
of Jesus—a life brimming with peace. This life has replaced the
unrest of my soul, healed the fractures in my mind, and restored
harmony to my relationships.

Today, I receive that life afresh for myself and my household. Let it
course through every weary place, revitalizing our faith, our hope,
and our love. Let it drive out the poison of anxiety, the sickness of
fear, and the strain of division.

Lord, this life is indestructible, unstoppable, and eternal. It is our
inheritance, purchased at the altar of the cross. As we abide in this
life, peace flows without ceasing, saturating every word we speak,
every step we take, and every connection we share.

In Jesus' name, Amen.

DAY 29

LIVING IN KINGDOM PEACE

"For God's Kingdom is not eating and drinking, but righteousness, peace, and joy in the Holy Spirit."
— Romans 14:17 WEB

Righteous King, I step into the reality of Your Kingdom—one where peace reigns, joy overflows, and righteousness stands immovable. This is the inheritance purchased for me through the blood of Jesus, and I claim it for myself and my family today.

Let kingdom peace govern our home, making it a sanctuary where Your Spirit is welcome and Your will is done. Let kingdom joy strengthen our hearts and keep our relationships full of life.

We refuse to live by the lesser systems of this world. Our atmosphere is the atmosphere of Heaven, our security is the blood, and our peace is unshakable. In this Kingdom, fear has no throne, chaos has no crown, and the enemy has no say.

In Jesus' name, Amen.

DAY 30

SANCTIFIED BY THE GOD OF PEACE

"May the God of peace himself sanctify you completely. May your whole spirit, soul, and body be preserved blameless at the coming of our Lord Jesus Christ."
— 1 Thessalonians 5:23 WEB

God of Peace, I welcome Your sanctifying work in every part of me. Through the blood of Jesus, cleanse my spirit, steady my soul, and strengthen my body. Leave no anxious thought, no fearful feeling, and no restless place untouched by Your peace.

Lord, let this same sanctifying power cover my family. May we be wholly set apart—our minds guarded, our emotions healed, our bodies strengthened. Let peace be the seal upon us, a divine mark that we are Yours.

We choose to live preserved, protected, and perfected by Your peace until the day of Your appearing. Nothing missing, nothing broken, nothing stolen—only the fullness of shalom reigning in us.

In Jesus' name, Amen.

DAY 31

REST IN THE SHADOW OF THE CROSS

"In peace I will both lay myself down and sleep, for you alone, Yahweh, make me live in safety."
— Psalm 4:8 WEB

O Lord, my Shield and my Peace, I thank You for the blood of Jesus that speaks a better word over my nights. I declare that every restless thought, every anxiety, and every midnight terror is stilled by the power of His cross. Your covenant blood covers my household like a warm blanket of divine safety, shutting the door to every harassing spirit.

I decree over myself and my family that our beds shall be altars of rest, not battlegrounds of the mind. The blood of Jesus has silenced the accuser, and His peace now reigns in our hearts and minds. Even as we close our eyes, angels stand guard at our doors, and the Prince of Peace lays His hand upon our heads.

Lord, because of the blood, I reject insomnia, fear, and dread. I receive holy rest as a gift purchased at Calvary. We shall awaken refreshed, strengthened, and filled with joy, knowing that our lives are hidden in Christ. No disturbance, no noise, no invisible storm can steal this rest. We lie down in peace, and we rise in peace. In Jesus' name, Amen.

DAY 32

COVERED IN PEACEFUL PROTECTION

"The blood shall be to you for a token on the houses where you are; and when I see the blood, I will pass over you, and no plague will be on you to destroy you..."
— Exodus 12:13 WEB

Mighty Deliverer, I lift my voice in gratitude for the blood of the Lamb that speaks mercy over my home. By this blood, every plague, sickness, and calamity is forbidden to cross our threshold. I declare that my family is sealed in covenant protection, hidden in the cleft of the Rock.

Father, Your Word assures me that peace is my portion because protection is my inheritance. No disease, no sudden disaster, and no work of darkness shall overtake us. The blood of Jesus is the mark that Heaven recognizes and Hell fears. I rest in the truth that the destroyer cannot pass through the door where the blood is applied.

I declare peace within our walls and safety in our dwelling places. Every assignment of harm is canceled, every snare is broken, and every demonic entry point is closed. The blood has spoken, and its voice thunders: "Peace!" Over my children, my spouse, my household, and all that concerns us, divine peace reigns like a fortress. In Jesus' name, Amen.

DAY 33

Pardon That Calms the Soul

"...for this is my blood of the new covenant, which is poured out for many for the remission of sins."
— Matthew 26:28 WEB

Loving Redeemer, I lift my hands in awe of the blood poured out for my complete pardon. Because of this covenant, shame is silenced, guilt is erased, and peace flows like a river into my heart. Every failure, every regret, and every dark memory bows to the authority of the cross.

Lord, I declare over myself and my family that we are forgiven, fully and forever. The record of wrongs has been washed away, and the accusing voices are muted. We will not live under the shadow of condemnation, for the blood of Jesus has brought us into the light of Your love.

Let emotional storms be calmed right now. Let troubled consciences be soothed. Let strained hearts exhale the breath of relief. By the blood, I choose to embrace peace—not as a distant hope, but as a present reality. Our home will be a sanctuary where forgiveness reigns, joy flourishes, and love is restored. In Jesus' name, Amen.

DAY 34

BREAKING THE CURSE'S GRIP

"Christ redeemed us from the curse of the law, having
become a curse for us…"
— Galatians 3:13 WEB

Chain-Breaking Savior, I stand in the victory of the cross and declare that every generational curse is shattered by the blood of Jesus. Mental torment, cycles of fear, depression, and confusion have no legal right to remain in me or my family.

By the authority of the blood, I uproot every inherited bondage and declare that the blessing of Abraham rests on our minds. I renounce every lie that says we are bound to repeat the failures of the past. The curse has been removed, and in its place, peace like a river floods our hearts and thoughts.

Lord, I receive the renewing of the mind for myself and my household. Every dark cloud is dispersed, every tormenting thought is silenced, and clarity comes. We shall walk in soundness of mind, strength of heart, and wholeness of soul. The blood of Jesus has spoken freedom, and we will not return to chains. In Jesus' name, Amen.

DAY 35

FREEDOM FROM THE INNER PRISON

"As for you also, because of the blood of your covenant, I have set free your prisoners from the pit in which there is no water."
— Zechariah 9:11 WEB

Delivering King, I worship You for the power of the blood that breaks the locks of inner captivity. I declare that every prison of fear, grief, and despair in my life and in my family is opened now.

Lord, You have called us out of dry, barren places into the well-watered gardens of Your peace. By the blood, I speak freedom over every heart weighed down by heaviness, over every soul trapped in memories of pain. The prison doors swing wide, and we step into the light of Your joy.

No longer shall we be bound by silent tears or unspoken sorrow. The chains have fallen, and the pit has lost its hold. We receive the liberty of the children of God, walking in the freedom purchased at Calvary. The blood has made us free indeed. In Jesus' name, Amen.

DAY 36

HEALING FOR THE BROKEN HEART

"He heals the broken in heart, and binds up their wounds."
— Psalm 147:3 WEB

Compassionate Healer, I lift my heart before You, trusting in the power of the blood to bind up every wound. Lord, where there has been betrayal, loss, or rejection, let the soothing balm of Calvary's love flow freely.

I declare over my family that every shattered heart is being mended stitch by stitch with cords of divine love. The blood of Jesus wipes away the stains of sorrow, closing the breaches left by pain. No wound is too deep for the Great Physician, and no scar is beyond His touch.

Lord, replace the ache with assurance, the grief with gladness, and the turmoil with tranquility. Let peace reign where pain once dwelled, and let joy overflow where mourning had a seat. In the blood, there is healing, and today we embrace it fully. In Jesus' name, Amen.

DAY 37

PEACE IN RECONCILIATION

"But all things are of God, who reconciled us to himself through Jesus Christ, and gave to us the ministry of reconciliation."
— 2 Corinthians 5:18 WEB

Father of Mercy, I thank You for reconciling me to Yourself through the blood of Jesus. Because I have peace with You, I declare peace in every relationship connected to my life and my family.

Lord, by this covenant, I break the power of offense, bitterness, and division. Let every wall that separates hearts be torn down. Where misunderstandings have grown roots, let truth and love uproot them. The blood of reconciliation speaks unity, and I declare that we shall walk in its power.

Make our home a dwelling of harmony, where the love of Christ is our language and peace is our atmosphere. Restore the bridges that have burned, and mend the ties that have frayed. We embrace the ministry of reconciliation and walk in the joy of restored fellowship. In Jesus' name, Amen.

DAY 38

CLEANSED FROM GUILT'S GRIP

"According to the law, nearly everything is cleansed with blood, and apart from shedding of blood there is no remission."
— Hebrews 9:22 WEB

Holy God, I thank You that the blood of Jesus has cleansed me and my family from every stain of sin. The heavy yoke of guilt is broken, and peace floods the places where shame once lived.

Lord, I refuse to carry burdens that the cross has already lifted. The voice of accusation is silenced, and the courtroom of Heaven has ruled us free. We are not condemned; we are cleansed. We are not stained; we are spotless by the blood.

Let this cleansing open the door for complete emotional healing. Let our hearts rest in the truth that nothing stands between us and Your presence. We walk in peace, we breathe in peace, and we live in the joy of the forgiven. In Jesus' name, Amen.

DAY 39

PEACE AS GOD'S PURCHASED POSSESSION

"Take heed, therefore, to yourselves and to all the flock, in which the Holy Spirit has made you overseers, to shepherd the assembly of the Lord and God which he purchased with his own blood."
— Acts 20:28 WEB

Righteous Father, I rejoice that I am not my own—I was bought with a price, the precious blood of Jesus. My worth is not determined by the world but by the value You placed on me.

I declare over my family that we are God's treasured possession, carried close to His heart. Because we belong to You, no evil can snatch us from Your hand, and no storm can unsettle our peace. The blood that purchased us has also sealed us, and that seal cannot be broken.

Lord, let our identity in You become the anchor of our souls. Let peace be the fruit of knowing we are wanted, chosen, and eternally loved. We will not live in fear of abandonment or rejection, for the One who bought us will keep us forever. In Jesus' name, Amen.

DAY 40

PEACE IN THE FAMILY CIRCLE

"...and might reconcile them both in one body to God
through the cross, having killed the hostility through it."
— Ephesians 2:16 WEB

Prince of Peace, I thank You for the cross that ends hostility and restores harmony. I speak Your blood-bought reconciliation into every strained relationship in my family.

Lord, where there has been distance, let there be closeness. Where there has been anger, let forgiveness flow. Where coldness has settled in, let the warmth of love return. The blood of Jesus has ended the war and signed the treaty of peace over our home.

I declare that our conversations will be seasoned with grace, our disagreements clothed with understanding, and our fellowship marked by joy. Let the peace of Christ reign over our meals, our gatherings, and our everyday moments. By the power of the cross, our family stands united in love. In Jesus' name, Amen.

DAY 41

Peaceful Life Through Righteous Blood

The work of righteousness will be peace, and the effect of
righteousness, quietness and confidence forever.
— Isaiah 32:17 WEB

Righteous King, I thank You for clothing me and my household in
the robe of righteousness purchased by the blood of Your Son.
Because of that holy blood, the verdict over my life is no longer
condemnation but divine acquittal. I decree that the righteousness
of Christ works in us today, producing a peace that cannot be
shattered and a quietness that storms cannot disturb.

By the power of the cross, I silence every voice of accusation, fear,
and unrest that would war against our minds. The righteousness
imputed to us becomes a shield, and the peace it produces becomes
a river flowing through our home, our relationships, and our inner
thoughts. Every hidden anxiety must bow to the Prince of Peace
who reigns in our midst.

Lord, let this confidence in Your finished work be unshakable.
Cause our lives to radiate the calm authority of those who know
they stand blameless before You. May our very atmosphere testify
that righteousness bears fruit in peace, and that our home is a
sanctuary under the crimson covering of Christ's sacrifice. In Jesus'
name, Amen.

DAY 42

HOPE AND PEACE

Now may the God of hope fill you with all joy and peace
in believing, that you may abound in hope, in the power
of the Holy Spirit.
— Romans 15:13 WEB

God of all hope, I lift my heart before You, cleansed and opened by
the blood of Jesus. You are the source of every pure joy and the
fountain of unshakable peace. Through the covenant of the cross,
You have made room in my spirit for the overflow of divine
expectation.

Today, I declare that my family and I are vessels for Your peace.
Every trace of despair, discouragement, and heaviness is expelled
by the life-giving power of Your Spirit. The blood that was shed on
Calvary dismantles hopelessness and makes way for a supernatural
confidence in Your promises. Joy rises like the morning sun in our
hearts, breaking the grip of night.

Lord, let Your peace settle deep in our minds, not as a fleeting
feeling but as a governing force. May hope overflow in us until it
touches every relationship, every decision, and every season of life.
We are rooted in the unchanging truth that the God of hope has
filled us and will keep filling us. In Jesus' name, Amen.

DAY 43

Channel of Peace

The fruit of righteousness is sown in peace by those who make peace.
— James 3:18 WEB

Lord of the Harvest, I thank You that the blood of Jesus has made me a sower of peace in a world of conflict. Because I am redeemed, I will plant seeds of righteousness in the soil of peace, knowing that what is sown in the Spirit will bear eternal fruit.

Let my words, my actions, and my very presence release the fragrance of Christ wherever I go. The cross has reconciled me to God and to others; therefore, I will not allow strife, bitterness, or division to take root in my home or in my heart. The peace of the covenant flows through me like a living river, nurturing every relationship and calming every storm.

Holy Spirit, make my family a living testimony that the work of the blood produces harmony. Let our lives become fertile ground where peace multiplies, influencing generations yet to come. May we walk as peacemakers who carry the authority of the cross, turning hearts toward righteousness. In Jesus' name, Amen.

DAY 44

Peace with Enemies

When a man's ways please Yahweh, he makes even his
enemies to be at peace with him.
— Proverbs 16:7 WEB

Faithful God, I stand under the cleansing stream of Jesus' blood and
align my ways with Your will. Because of this covenant, my life is
pleasing in Your sight—not by my merit, but by the righteousness
of Christ. You have promised that such a life causes even enemies
to live in peace with us.

I declare that every source of contention, hostility, and hidden
attack is silenced in the presence of the Lord. The blood of the Lamb
speaks a better word over my relationships, canceling the power of
vengeance and hostility. Every demonic agenda to stir conflict is
dismantled by the authority of the cross.

Lord, surround my family with Your shield of favor. Cause even
those who once opposed us to walk in civility, respect, and peace.
Let Your presence in our lives disarm hostility and establish us in
supernatural rest. May our ways continually please You, drawing
even adversaries into the sphere of Your reconciling power. In Jesus'
name, Amen.

DAY 45

THE RULING PEACE OF CHRIST'S BLOOD

And let the peace of Christ rule in your hearts, to which
also you were called in one body, and be thankful.
— Colossians 3:15 WEB

Prince of Peace, I yield the throne of my heart to You alone. By the
blood of Your cross, You have purchased my peace, and I refuse to
let any other ruler occupy this sacred place. Your peace is not a
suggestion—it is the ruling authority over my mind, my emotions,
and my household.

I decree that anxiety, fear, and agitation are dethroned in my life.
Every disturbance bows to the reigning peace of Christ. My family
and I walk in the calling of unity, joined together under one
covenant and one Spirit. Gratitude rises in us like incense, for we
know this peace is not earned but given through the sacrifice of the
Lamb.

Lord, let this ruling peace govern our decisions, our conversations,
and our responses. Make our hearts a sanctuary where Your calm
reigns unchallenged. May the world see the evidence of Your
lordship in the stability of our spirits. In Jesus' name, Amen.

DAY 46

PEACE THROUGH OBEDIENCE BY GRACE

Those who love your law have great peace. Nothing causes
them to stumble.
— Psalm 119:165 WEB

Holy Lawgiver, I bless You for the grace that enables me to love Your
Word. The blood of Jesus has written Your law on my heart, turning
obedience from a burden into a joy. Because I love Your commands,
You promise me great peace that the world cannot steal.

I declare that stumbling is not my portion. Every trap of offense,
confusion, or distraction is rendered powerless by my devotion to
Your truth. My household walks in the unshakable peace that
comes from aligning our lives with Your will. The Word is our
anchor, and the blood is our covering.

Lord, let our love for Your law grow daily. Cause our thoughts to be
shaped by Scripture, and our steps to be steady upon the path of
righteousness. May our obedience draw us deeper into covenant
rest, where nothing has the power to cause us to fall. In Jesus' name,
Amen.

DAY 47

SET APART FROM EMOTIONAL CHAOS

By which will we have been sanctified through the offering
of the body of Jesus Christ once for all.
— Hebrews 10:10 WEB

Sanctifying Lord, I thank You for the once-for-all sacrifice of Jesus' body and blood. That holy offering has set me and my family apart—not just from sin, but from the chaos, confusion, and turmoil that dominate this world.

By covenant right, I declare that our emotions are under the sanctifying power of the cross. Fear, despair, and instability have no hold on us. We are a consecrated people, chosen to live in peace even in a troubled world. Your Spirit guards our hearts, and Your blood seals our minds in stability.

Lord, keep us in this sanctified place, where Your presence defines our reality and Your peace shapes our atmosphere. Let the world see in us a calm that cannot be shaken, a joy that cannot be stolen, and a stability rooted in the blood of the covenant. In Jesus' name, Amen.

DAY 48

Peace in Knowing Sin Has Been Removed

> But now once at the end of the ages, he has been revealed
> to put away sin by the sacrifice of himself.
> — Hebrews 9:26 WEB

Redeeming Savior, I praise You for the eternal work of the cross. Once and for all, You put away sin—not in part, but in full. This finished work brings me peace beyond measure, for I know that guilt, shame, and condemnation have no voice over my life.

I declare that my family and I walk in the freedom of complete forgiveness. The blood of Jesus has erased the record against us, silencing every whisper of the accuser. Our hearts are light, our minds are clear, and our relationships are restored because the barrier of sin has been forever removed.

Lord, let the reality of this redemption sink deeper each day. May we live as those truly forgiven, with no shadow of the past clouding our peace. Let joy and rest fill our home as we stand in the light of Your finished work. In Jesus' name, Amen.

DAY 49

RECEIVING THE MIND OF CHRIST

Have this in your mind, which was also in Christ Jesus.
— Philippians 2:5 WEB

Lord of Glory, I thank You that through the blood of Jesus, I am not left to think as the world thinks. You have given me the mind of Christ—a mind rooted in humility, truth, and peace. This mind shapes my thoughts, my reactions, and my vision for life.

I decree that my household rejects the patterns of fear, pride, and unrest that dominate this age. The cross has renewed our minds, aligning us with the heart of the Savior. Every anxious thought is replaced with calm wisdom; every impulse toward strife is subdued by Your peace.

Lord, let this Christ-mind be evident in our speech, our choices, and our relationships. May we think Your thoughts, speak Your truth, and walk in Your ways, bearing witness to the transforming power of the covenant. In Jesus' name, Amen.

DAY 50

A Calm Life Through Christ's Presence

Now may the Lord of peace himself give you peace at all
times in all ways. The Lord be with you all.
— 2 Thessalonians 3:16 WEB

Lord of Peace, I open the doors of my life and my home to You. By Your blood, You have purchased the right to dwell with us, and Your presence is the atmosphere where peace reigns.

I declare that we receive peace at all times and in every situation. Whether the winds of change blow fiercely or the path is calm, Your presence steadies our steps. The blood of the Lamb stands between us and every storm, commanding stillness to every wave that rises against us.

Lord, walk through the rooms of our home. Fill each space with the fragrance of Your peace. Let Your nearness be the comfort that guards our hearts, the light that dispels our fears, and the strength that holds us steady. We welcome You fully, knowing that where You are, no storm can prevail. In Jesus' name, Amen.

DAY 51

PEACE SEALED BY THE BLOOD

"Moses took the blood, and sprinkled it on the people, and said, 'Behold, the blood of the covenant, which Yahweh has made with you concerning all these words.'"
— Exodus 24:8 WEB

O Covenant-Keeping God, I stand beneath the crimson covering of the blood of Jesus and declare that my peace is not fragile—it is sealed by the eternal Word and the unbreakable covenant of the cross. Your blood has spoken a better word over me and my household, silencing every storm, breaking every chain, and marking us as untouchable to the adversary.

Today, I decree that the same voice that thundered at Sinai and confirmed Your promises through the shedding of blood now resounds over my life. My mind will not be tormented. My emotions will not be tossed by the winds of fear. My relationships will not be fractured by the schemes of the enemy. We are anchored in the covenant of peace that cannot be annulled.

Let every storm in my home bow to the blood. Let every anxiety dissolve in the assurance of Your oath. We walk in the safety of Your unshakable word, our hearts resting in the security of Your promises. Our peace is not a temporary feeling—it is a divine inheritance sealed forever by the blood of Christ. In Jesus' name, Amen.

DAY 52

GRACE TO LIVE PEACEABLY

"If it is possible, as much as it is up to you, be at peace with
all men."
— Romans 12:18 WEB

Prince of Peace, You have empowered me by the blood of Your Son
to walk in peace even in the most difficult places. My capacity to
love, forgive, and remain calm in the midst of hostility does not
come from my own strength, but from the victory of the cross that
has already conquered every spirit of division and strife.

I declare that my home will be a sanctuary of peace, even when the
world rages. You have given me grace to respond with gentleness,
to disarm anger with kindness, and to pursue reconciliation as a
living testimony of the gospel. I refuse to be drawn into the snares
of offense or the traps of bitterness.

Lord, let the fragrance of Your peace saturate my speech, my
actions, and my relationships. Even where others reject it, I will
remain steadfast, because my peace flows from the blood that
bought me. My family will be known as peacemakers, shining in a
world desperate for rest. In Jesus' name, Amen.

DAY 53

Rescued from Inner Turmoil

"He has redeemed my soul in peace from the battle that
was against me, although there are many who oppose me."
— Psalm 55:18 WEB

Redeemer of my soul, I lift my voice in triumph because You have
not only redeemed me, but You have done it in peace. No battle
within or without can steal the calm You have placed in my spirit.
Though many may rise against me, they will stumble and fall, for
the blood has purchased my freedom from inner war.

I release every weight, every anxious thought, and every unhealed
wound into Your hands. The storms of the mind have been silenced
by the voice that cried, "It is finished!" I declare that no accusation,
no betrayal, no unseen warfare will unsettle my peace.

Today, my household and I stand in the quiet strength of Your
covenant. The noise of the enemy is drowned out by the song of the
redeemed. You have lifted me above the chaos, set me in a place of
rest, and wrapped me in the stillness of Your presence. In Jesus'
name, Amen.

DAY 54

Surrendering to Peace

"Acquaint yourself with him now, and be at peace. By it, good will come to you."
— Job 22:21 WEB

Holy Father, I lay my will, my plans, and my anxious striving at Your feet. To know You is to know peace, and to walk with You is to walk in quiet strength. I choose agreement with Your Word over the noise of my own understanding.

I surrender the battles of my mind and the storms of my emotions. Your blood has given me access to a covenant where my soul can breathe again. In yielding to Your way, I find not loss, but abundance; not defeat, but blessing.

Let my home be a place where Your peace rules as King. Let my decisions flow from the counsel of Your Spirit. As I align my heart with Yours, let every area of my life be filled with the goodness that comes from walking hand in hand with the God of peace. In Jesus' name, Amen.

DAY 55

PEACE THROUGH THE LIVING WORD

"This is my comfort in my affliction, for your word has revived me."
— Psalm 119:50 WEB

Faithful Shepherd, in the valley of trouble, Your Word breathes life into my soul. The blood of Jesus has unlocked every promise, making it my right to stand in unshakable peace. Though afflictions may press on every side, Your living Word revives my hope and strengthens my heart.

I refuse to feed on the lies of fear or the whispers of defeat. Instead, I feast on the truth that cannot be broken. Your voice stills my anxious thoughts, and the revelation of the cross drives out every shadow.

In my family, Your Word will be our anchor. We will speak it, pray it, and stand on it until peace overflows in every room. We are not defined by what we see, but by what You have spoken. In Jesus' name, Amen.

DAY 56

CLEANSED FOR MENTAL STABILITY

"They washed their robes, and made them white in the Lamb's blood."
— Revelation 7:14 WEB

Spotless Lamb, I thank You that my identity is no longer stained by the past, but washed and made pure through Your blood. Because I am clean, my mind is no longer bound by the shame, confusion, and torment that once ruled me.

I declare that every lie of unworthiness is broken, every voice of condemnation silenced. Your blood has given me a new name, a new mind, and a new peace that nothing can shake. My home will not be a place of mental torment but of renewed thoughts anchored in truth.

Let the clarity of heaven fill my heart. Let the confidence of being fully forgiven steady my emotions. As I walk in this cleansed identity, I will not return to the garments of guilt, but remain clothed in the white robes of righteousness and peace. In Jesus' name, Amen.

DAY 57

HEALING FROM EMOTIONAL PAIN

"Surely he has borne our sickness and carried our suffering..."
— Isaiah 53:4 WEB

Man of Sorrows, acquainted with grief, I worship You for carrying what I could not bear. Every weight of anxiety, every crushing sadness, every silent pain has been nailed to the cross. Your blood speaks healing over the wounds no one sees.

I choose to release my grip on pain and embrace the wholeness You purchased. You did not only take my sin, You took my sorrow. You bore the heaviness so my heart could be light. You carried the weight so my family could be free from cycles of fear and depression.

Let Your peace saturate every memory that once brought torment. Let Your presence breathe life into the places within me that felt dead. From this day forward, I will walk in the joy and rest that are my inheritance in the blood. In Jesus' name, Amen.

DAY 58

PEACE AND RIGHTEOUSNESS UNITED

"Mercy and truth meet together. Righteousness and peace
have kissed each other."
— Psalm 85:10 WEB

God of Covenant Harmony, I thank You that in the blood of Jesus,
righteousness and peace are forever joined. Because of the cross, I
am not striving for acceptance; I live from it. Peace is the fruit of
knowing I am justified in Your sight.

I declare that the rule of righteousness brings stability to my
thoughts, unity to my family, and calm to my relationships. There
is no separation between my standing before You and the rest of my
soul—You have made them one.

May my home be an expression of this divine union, where truth is
spoken in love, mercy flows freely, and peace reigns without end. In
Jesus' name, Amen.

DAY 59

WALKING IN THE GOSPEL OF PEACE

"How beautiful are the feet of those who preach the Good
News of peace…"
— Romans 10:15 WEB

Lord of the Harvest, thank You for calling me to carry the message
of peace, not just in words, but in the life I live. Through the blood,
I have received this peace, and now I am commissioned to spread
it wherever my feet go.

I declare that my steps will not bring confusion, but clarity; not
strife, but reconciliation. My family and I will walk as living
testimonies of the peace purchased by Christ, becoming vessels of
healing in a fractured world.

Let our presence bring calm to chaos, and our words be rivers of
life. May the fragrance of the gospel be evident in every interaction,
opening hearts to the One who made peace through the blood of
His cross. In Jesus' name, Amen.

DAY 60

RESURRECTION PEACE EVERY DAY

"When therefore it was evening, on that day, the first day
of the week, and when the doors were locked... Jesus came
and stood in the middle, and said to them, 'Peace be to
you.'"
— John 20:19 WEB

Risen Lord, I welcome You into the locked places of my life. Your
blood has opened the way for You to step into every room of my
heart, every hidden fear, and every closed-off relationship,
declaring, "Peace be to you."

I receive that peace now—peace that does not depend on
circumstances, peace that cannot be stolen by threats or storms.
Just as You breathed it over Your disciples, breathe it over my family
and me today.

Let Your resurrection life displace despair. Let Your presence
dismantle fear. May every day begin and end with the assurance
that You stand among us, and where You stand, peace reigns
unchallenged. In Jesus' name, Amen.

EPILOGUE

You have now prayed through sixty days of prophetic declarations anchored in the blood of Jesus Christ. This journey was not simply about learning new prayers—it was about re-establishing the truth that your peace is not circumstantial. It is covenantal. It cannot be revoked, and it does not expire.

Perhaps along the way, you noticed subtle changes—a calmer response where anxiety once ruled, a softened heart in a strained relationship, a deep stillness during what would normally be a stressful moment. These are not coincidences. They are the fruit of enforcing your blood-bought inheritance.

In John 16:33, Jesus said, *"In the world you have oppression; but cheer up! I have overcome the world."* This means you will still encounter storms, but the storms no longer have the right to dictate your inner condition. You are hidden in Christ, washed in His blood, and guarded by His peace.

Let these 60 days be the beginning of a lifestyle. Keep the prayers close. Speak them in times of trouble and in seasons of rest. Let your home, workplace, and relationships become living testimonies of what it means to be a covenant child who walks in *shalom*.

The blood still speaks. It speaks forgiveness, it speaks victory, and it speaks peace. Now that you have received it afresh, walk boldly into every day with this unshakable truth in your heart: the covenant has been signed in blood, and the peace of God is yours forever.

Encourage Others with Your Story

If this prayer guide has strengthened your faith, deepened your intercession, or helped you stand in the gap, would you consider leaving a short review on Amazon? Your feedback not only encourages others but also helps more believers discover this resource and join in the prayer movement. Every review—just a few sentences—makes a difference and helps spread the call to command the evening. Thank you for being part of this movement.

MORE FROM PRAYERSCRIPTS

PARDON THROUGH THE BLOOD:

60 DAYS OF PRAYERS FOR TOTAL FORGIVENESS AND FREEDOM

Guilt is a prison. The blood of Jesus holds the key.

Pardon Through the Blood invites you on a 60-day journey into the liberating power of Christ's sacrifice—a sacred cleansing that reaches deeper than shame, regret, or condemnation. If you've ever felt stuck in cycles of failure, haunted by your past, or burdened by hidden sin, this book is your roadmap to lasting forgiveness and spiritual freedom. Each day offers a blood-specific Scripture, a focused prayer theme, and a prophetic, Spirit-filled prayer that will help you boldly approach God's mercy seat. You'll experience what it means to be fully forgiven, deeply cleansed, and restored to right relationship with the Father—all through the blood of Jesus.

PROTECTION THROUGH THE BLOOD:

60 DAYS OF PRAYERS FOR LIVING UNTOUCHABLE UNDER CHRIST'S BLOOD

You are not helpless. You are not exposed. You are covered— completely—by the blood of Jesus.

In a world of rising dangers, demonic assaults, and spiritual unpredictability, Protection Through the Blood equips you and your family to live untouchable under the supernatural shield of Christ's blood. Every day's entry is a power-packed prayer experience rooted in Scripture—designed to build a blood-line barrier around your life, home, and destiny.. Part of *The Blood Covenant Series*, this second volume is a must-have companion for believers who refuse to live defenseless in a dark world. If you're ready to activate heaven's strongest defense system and stand boldly in the shadow of the Almighty, this 60-day journey is for you.

Live bold. Live covered. Live untouchable—through the blood.

PREVAIL THROUGH THE BLOOD:

60 DAYS OF PRAYERS FOR SPIRITUAL MASTERY OVER THE ENEMY

What if every scheme of the enemy against your life could be dismantled—by one unstoppable weapon?

In *Prevail Through the Blood*, you'll discover how to wield the most powerful force in the universe—the Blood of Jesus Christ—to overcome every spiritual assault, shatter generational yokes, and walk in daily victory. This is more than a prayer book. It is your 60-day spiritual war manual, designed to train your hands for battle and your heart for triumph. This third installment in The Blood Covenant Series invites you into a journey of spiritual mastery. Whether you are in the heat of battle or standing in victory, every page will sharpen your discernment, stir your faith, and saturate your home in the protective power of Christ's blood.

Break free from every chain. Pray with fire. Win with the Blood.

PRESERVATION THROUGH THE BLOOD:

60 DAYS OF PRAYERS FOR DIVINE HEALING AND WHOLENESS

Unlock Lasting Healing and Wholeness Through the Blood of Jesus

Preservation Through the Blood: 60 Days of Prayers for Divine Healing and Wholeness is your prophetic, Scripture-packed guide to receiving total restoration in your body, soul, and spirit through the covenant power of Christ's blood. More than a devotional, this book is a healing altar—built on 60 carefully selected Bible verses that directly reveal God's will to heal and preserve you.

Whether you're battling chronic illness, emotional trauma, lingering symptoms, or generational afflictions, these blood-based prayers will speak directly to the root of the issue to appropriate divine healing. This book equips you to confront the source, not just the symptoms.

PROSPERITY THROUGH THE BLOOD:

60 DAYS OF PRAYERS FOR UNLOCKING HEAVEN'S WEALTH AND WALKING IN COVENANT INCREASE

You were redeemed for more than survival—
you were redeemed to prosper.

In a world filled with economic uncertainty, God's promise of abundance still stands. *Prosperity Through the Blood: 60 Days of Prayers for Unlocking Heaven's Wealth and Walking in Covenant Increase* invites you into a powerful journey of discovering what the blood of Jesus truly purchased for you—not just eternal life, but a full, flourishing, and prosperous life on earth. Whether you're in a season of financial need or simply hungry to experience more of what belongs to you in Christ, *Prosperity Through the Blood* is your roadmap to living untouchable, unshakable, and abundantly blessed under the power of the blood.

COMMAND YOUR MORNING: 30 DAYS OF PRAYERS AND DECLARATIONS TO SEIZE YOUR DAY AND SHAPE YOUR DESTINY

There is a battle over every morning—and every believer must choose to either drift into the day or command it.

Command Your Morning: 30 Days of Prayers and Declarations to Seize Your Day and Shape Your Destiny is a spiritually charged guide to help you start each day with purpose, power, and prophetic clarity. This is more than a devotional—it's a call to action. Each day in this 30-day journey is built around **five core biblical themes** that set the spiritual tone for your day: **Praise, Purpose, Protection, Provision** and **Position**. Don't just wake up. Command your morning—and shape your destiny.

COMMAND YOUR NIGHT: 30 DAYS OF PRAYERS AND DECLARATIONS TO SECURE YOUR REST AND SHAPE YOUR TOMORROW

Every night is a spiritual battlefield—what you do before you sleep can determine the course of your tomorrow.

Command Your Night: 30 Days of Prayers and Declarations to Secure Your Rest and Shape Your Tomorrow is a powerful devotional prayer manual designed to help you end each day in victory, not vulnerability. Whether you're battling anxiety, spiritual attacks, restlessness, or simply longing for deeper peace, this book equips you to reclaim your night with bold, Scripture-rooted prayers. Each night is structured around five strategic prayer themes: *Shut, Shield, Silence, Show, Sleep.*

COMMAND YOUR EVENING: 30 DAYS OF PRAYERS AND DECLARATIONS TO RELEASE THE DAY AND RECLAIM INTIMACY WITH GOD

There is a battle over every transition—and evening is one of the most spiritually neglected.

Command Your Evening is the third book in the **Command Your Destiny** series—following *Command Your Morning* and *Command Your Night*. In heaven's rhythm, the evening is not just a wind-down—it's a window. A sacred hour where destinies are recalibrated, burdens are lifted, and hearts are re-centered in the presence of God. In *Command Your Evening*, you'll journey through 30 days of intentional, Spirit-led prayers and prophetic declarations centered around five key evening themes: **Release, Renew, Refocus, Rebuild,** and **Rest.**

Scriptures & Prayers for Deliverance from Trouble: 40 Days of Prayer for When Life Feels Overwhelming

Are you walking through a season where life feels heavy, hope feels distant, and your prayers feel weak?

Scriptures & Prayers for Deliverance from Trouble is a 40-day journey of honest prayers and powerful Scriptures to help you find peace, strength, and healing when life is overwhelming. Each day offers a personal, Scripture-based prayer written in the language of real faith and raw trust. This devotional isn't about perfect words— it's about real connection with God when you need Him most.

Scriptures & Prayers for Deliverance from Evil:

50 Days of Prayer to Overcome Darkness and Find God's Protection

When darkness presses in, how do you pray?

When fear grips your heart or unseen battles rage around you, you need more than generic words—you need Scripture, truth, and the steady hand of God to lead you through.

Scriptures & Prayers for Deliverance from Evil: 50 Days of Prayer to Overcome Darkness and Find God's Protection is a powerful devotional journey designed to help you pray boldly and biblically through seasons of spiritual warfare, oppression, fear, or uncertainty.

Scriptures & Prayers for Engaging the Enemy:

70 Days of Prayer to Rebuke the Enemy and Release God's Power

You weren't called to run from the battle—

you were anointed to win it.

Scriptures & Prayers for Engaging the Enemy: 70 Days of Prayer to Rebuke the Enemy and Release God's Power is a bold devotional for believers who are ready to rise, resist, and reclaim what the enemy has tried to steal. If you're tired of feeling spiritually outnumbered, this book will equip you to fight back—with Scripture in your mouth and power in your prayers. Over 70 days, you'll be guided through five strategic phases of spiritual warfare: (1) Rebuking the Enemy, (2) Releasing Terror Upon the Enemy (3) Praying for the Fall of the Enemy (4) Treading Upon the Enemy (5) When Heaven Strikes.

The war is real. But so is your victory.

Scriptures & Prayers for Combating Spiritual Wickedness:

50 Days of Prayer to Overthrow Wicked Plans and Stand in God's Victory

Are you facing opposition that feels deeper than the natural? Do you sense hidden resistance working against your progress, peace, or purpose? You're not imagining it—and you're not powerless.

Rooted in the authority of Scripture and fueled by bold, targeted prayers, *Scriptures & Prayers for Combating Spiritual Wickedness* equips you to confront darkness head-on. Each day features a focused Bible passage and a heartfelt, Scripture-based prayer designed to nullify ungodly counsel, disrupt demonic schemes, and establish God's victory in every area of your life.

STANDING IN THE GAP FOR COVENANT AWAKENING:

30 DAYS OF PRAYER FOR NATIONAL REPENTANCE, RIGHTEOUS LEADERSHIP & GOD'S SOVEREIGN RULE

What if your prayers could help turn the tide of a nation?

America stands at a spiritual crossroads. Division deepens, truth is under siege, and righteousness is being redefined. But God is still searching for those who will stand in the gap—intercessors who will cry out for mercy, justice, and national awakening.

Standing in the Gap for Covenant Awakening is a 30-day prayer guide for believers who sense the urgency of the hour and long to see their nation return to God.

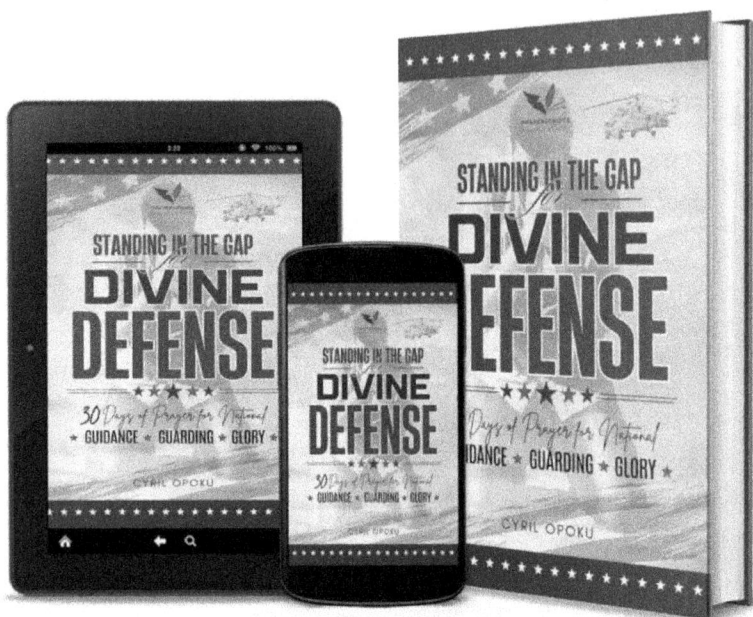

STANDING IN THE GAP FOR DIVINE DEFENSE:

30 DAYS OF PRAYER FOR NATIONAL GUIDANCE, GUARDING & GLORY

When the foundations of a nation feel as if they're shaking, prayer is the strongest fortress you can build.

Standing in the Gap for Divine Defense: 30 Days of Prayer for National Guidance, Guarding & Glory is your call to action—a 30-day journey of powerful, Scripture-rooted intercession that invites everyday believers to become watchmen on the walls for their nation. Drawing on timeless truths from God's Word, this devotional equips you to stand in the gap for your nation and **Seek Heaven's Wisdom, Secure Divine Protection,** and **Ignite Spiritual Awakening.** If you sense the urgency of the hour and long to see your country guided and guarded by the hand of God, open these pages. Stand in the gap. Watch Him move.

STANDING IN THE GAP FOR NATIONAL HEALING:

40 DAYS OF PRAYER FOR RECONCILIATION, RIGHTEOUSNESS, AND RESTORATION

What if your prayers could help heal a nation? What if God is waiting for someone—like you—to stand in the gap?

Standing in the Gap for National Healing: 40 Days of Prayer for Reconciliation, Righteousness, and Restoration is a bold, Spirit-filled call to action for believers who refuse to sit on the sidelines while their nation drifts further from God. In a time marked by division, confusion, and moral decline, this book equips you to pray with power, precision, and unshakable hope. Inside, you'll find 40 days of Scripture-based intercession divided into three strategic sections: **Peace, Unity & Reconciliation, Morality, Truth & Righteous Leadership**, and **National Restoration & Reformation**. It's time to stop watching history unfold—and start shaping it in prayer.

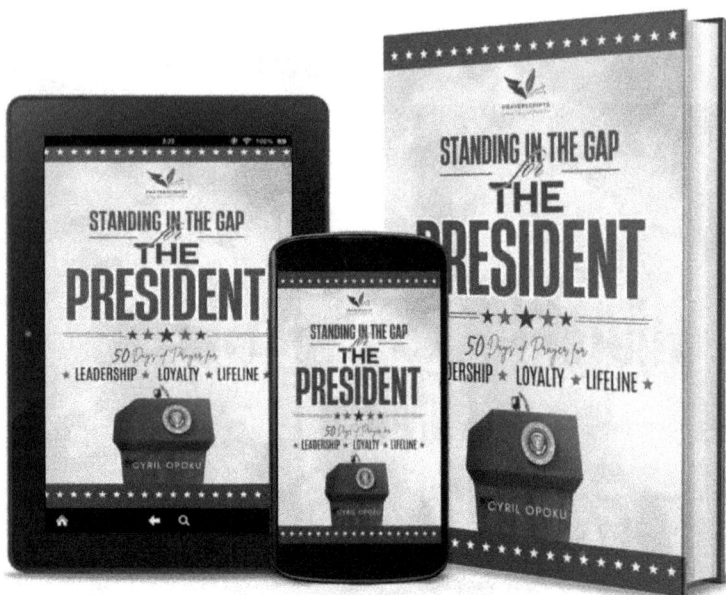

STANDING IN THE GAP FOR THE PRESIDENT:

50 DAYS OF PRAYER FOR LEADERSHIP, LOYALTY, AND LIFELINE

When a nation's leader is under spiritual siege, will you answer the call to stand in the gap?

Standing in the Gap for The President: 50 Days of Prayer for Leadership, Loyalty, and Lifeline is a bold, Scripture-saturated prayer guide for those who understand that the battles facing our leaders are more than political—they are spiritual. Assassination attempts, betrayal from within, and attacks on character and conscience are not just headlines—they're signs of the times. Inside, you'll find 50 days of strategic intercession divided into three high-impact sections: **Presidential Character & Leadership, Against Disloyal Insiders,** and **Against Assassination Attempts.** The future of a nation can shift through the prayers of the faithful. It's time to stand in the gap.

www.ingramcontent.com/pod-product-compliance
Lightning Source LLC
Chambersburg PA
CBHW062020040426
42447CB00010B/2082

*9 781988 439730 *